D1553435

Our

Mortal

Condition

Special thanks to my parents Brenda and Victor for being who they are, without their experiences I wouldn't experience the world as I do.

To Angie for helping me grow into who I've always been. For showing me a love I could never have thought to exist.

To everyone else who I've had the pleasure to meet. I love you. Nothing but gratitude. A piece of each of your lights are a part of me. My perspective broadened by your precious company.

To the universe, I'm beyond blessed to have the opportunity to exist freely.

Table of Contents

Reflections *33*

Preface

Who am I?

If that's not the hardest question in the world I really have no clue what is.

What trips me up is that we spend our entire lives with ourselves, and it still seems to be a mystery. The behaviors, actions, and things we seek. They must emerge from some place to become who we seem to be.

My first thought is my family, my DNA; the natural coding. I look like them, act like them, grew up with them. So maybe they can tell me something about us. How we emerge from the womb as blank slates and record every thing that our environment plays. I've always wanted to know why we say, act and do as we do, and luckily science has graciously uncovered some mechanistic clues.

What it comes down to is the nature vs nurture, the mistake is seeing them as separate because true understanding comes from the marriage of the two.

Our behaviors and actions come from the people we hold most true. Our desires and wills both products of the environment. How we view the world is entirely synonymous with the treatment of our consciousness. Habits built up on the notes we had taken from our childhood experiences. Not good nor bad all just interactions in the end. The basis of connections we make outside of our heads. Manifested by the connections we create within them.

Understanding the power to change your behavior must first come from a place of curiosity. To understand why you do anything. Before curiosity you must feel safe, because fears will take you far away from understanding and grace.

Fear is a natural mechanism that's been put in place to alert us of things that cause us pain. However just like behaviors fear is learned too, and how we interpret them is entirely up to you. All knowledge passed down to help you survive in a world where things die. Community teaches us all these things, because community is all that we hope to bring to the people we love and cherish. A place of comfort and understanding. Relatable characters to learn our lessons or laugh and inspire to further our missions. They teach us what to fear and the laws of which to adhere. Society is the collection of all those spheres.

The common laws of community, the common behaviors and fears. They force us into a road of life with markers and lines to keep us right. Ultimately there's no laws to life and the roads are nothing but a sample size of one way we should live our lives.

To truly appreciate and break away from the lies that you tell yourself each night about what you can't do. Understand that you're human and that process of thinking just isn't true. We are made in God's image and this isn't religious. We are capable of anything we are willing to witness. Self-belief is the philosophical principal of the universe and what you believe with your soul will find its place on this Earth. To achieve this capacity you must first come forth with humility and admiration of this condition we share, not just with each other but all living things because we are all susceptible to mortality.

The Collective Experience

Born, live, die.
All things that give us happiness, sadness,
meaning, and strife lay in between the
sandwich of life.
Birth to who we are, live to what we see
and die to who we've been.
Then the cycle begins again.

To say it'll be you is hard to know perhaps
it's the closest of kin or someone you've
been.
Our condition is topsy turvy.
The experience is most worthy.
Figuring out what we are meant to do will
always be top priority.

From the brightest to the fools, we are all
equal in this world of pools.
Vulnerable to each tide that pulls us into
our lives. To break free is the ultimate
dream. To wake up is to take hold of
reality.

Mortality

At some point in time, we will all die.
The guarantee of life.

You live so reserved.
Afraid to be free.
What is it then that hinders your peace?
Fear for what is already going to appear.

The gates will await you.

What will you bring?
Trinkets and tools.
That will be of no use.
They will disappear as the body that
harbors you.
Will return to dust, as it was before
you were conceived into this world.

A condition shared by all but one
Life itself.
The concept of love.

Behavior

You play your role very well from the hand
gestures to the words.
You've learned them fast.

Taught from the greatest class, if the
teachers were good is yet to be seen.

Your mannerisms and identity are not
what they seem.

Nothing becomes something from
nothing.
It has always been.
So tell me now, where does it begin?

From the love that lets us live.
Be it people, places, things.
If it brings us peace and sustenance to
some degree.
That is what we'll bleed.
The way we cope.
To make this better for ourselves we must
broaden our scope.
And see the world for what it is.
Filled with empty ideas fighting to exist.

Loneliness

Separation from a community of love.
Your family, friends, loved ones.
We long for their attention, the feeling of
their presence.

I can't help feeling so neglected.
When I don't get their affection.
It hurts in my soul, the deepest ache when
I'm alone.

Cherish the times we have with each
other.
We learn everything we know from one
another.
If you don't know where to find company.
Find a way into a community.
You'll discover it's the remedy.
To all those days of being lonely.

Depression

A restless mind can be a blessing.
Full of thoughts from the entire spectrum.
Thoughts of hope, and wonder.
To inner messages of eternal slumber

When happiness suffers from emotional
drought
Thoughts of doubt begin to sprout.

The point of existence, does it even
matter?
Existential crisis due to Earthly chatter.
Why live? Does anyone care?
Entertaining thoughts laced with despair.

Questioning your importance.
These feelings are misguided.
All you want to know is that you're not
making it harder for anyone to breathe.
If negativity is all you eat, then you can
expect reality to grow accordingly.

After wondering about who would cry for
you.
Even if you find it's none, one or two
That's more than enough to continue.

When you find yourself to be proud,
people will find ways to tear you down.
Don't allow your pride to impede on other
lives.
If you find it doesn't
Then love it.
Haters are just projecting.
Covet the things you find to be special.
Use them to make the world better.

Optimism

Are there dangers to being optimistic?

Some might say they can lead to
expectations that are unrealistic,
but optimism isn't what expects.
It's having an outlook that's bright in
respect.

Trials will come and go between now and
then.
Life is hard, but there is no disconnect
Between optimism and realistic intent.

It's not a matter of neglecting the negative
Its identifying that we have a choice
To stay in the shade or bask in the sun.
On a cold winter day tell me which is more
fun?

When it's hot and bright
Being in the shade keeps us cool
Because it's all about balance
Says every damned wise fool.

Joy

An energy within
One, you can't hide because your face just
gives you up.

This feeling reveals you like curtains on a
stage.
Exposing the play and all you must
entertain.

Brightness embodies you.
You shine.
The signs that you find.
Ways you interact with the people who
might lack.
The spark of happiness that doesn't slack.

More a state of being than a feeling.
Gratitude is good reasoning.
Happiness comes and goes but joy is more
interwoven in your whole.
Being the one in your tribe to start that
trend of feeling fine.
In a time where it's hard to appreciate the
things that bring elation.
A state of a nation.

All things can be delivered from decline
when we find it in our hearts.
To shock others with the same spark that
drives our smile.

If the situation remains, shift the
perspective.
Let's make it popular to share with each
other our affection and positive
intentions.

Enlightenment

To enlighten is to add
But you can't add to what is bright.
Instead be immersed in its light.

Don't be confused with the wisdom of
fools.
That claim to find balance in external
tools.
Feel what is right.
Be relinquished of your mind.
You might just realize that you've been
blind this whole time to the signs that tell
you what is and what is not.

At their core, all these signs are just
manifestations of thought.

Add to the Ambience

We just want to share with the world a
piece of our souls.
Let them know we alone cannot make the
world whole.

Like light in a room
Flowers in full bloom
Let our spirits spread life lest ignorance
bring doom.

A Good Life

Relationships
Passion
Reflection
and Action

Four fundamentals for a life of
satisfaction.

My martial art, the way of the soul
So it may be filled to the brim
Full, when I'm old
Let it spill over and fill any holes.
So the dreams and desires of the youth
make me whole.

Martial Art

The true way is the way of your own.
This martial art tears down
and makes whole
For you can't build if your foundation is
poor.
Find what to believe then start to soar.
If you believe in yourself, and trust in your
relationships
You can command this ship through
storms and trepidation.
Your worst fears should be never facing
them.

A samurai, full of honor and code
Wear your armor proudly
And dare to be bold
Wield the sword you forged through fire
and storms.
Swiftly cut down your enemies
Keeping a mind that's empty.
Embody what it means
To exceed the idea of possibility.

The Way of the Soul

Step one you must come to terms with
who you are.
If you are unsure don't fret too hard.
We are a process.
Our own magnum opus
So ask the hard questions.
Focus inwardly, and you might find the
answers you seek.
They might not be pleasant to see.
Perhaps terrifying and cruel,
but use it as a tool.
To level up the warrior in your heart.
This type of strength is one aspect of
God's art.

Step two is to pursue the dreams that exist
deep inside you.
It doesn't take much to dream, but the
challenge is making them true.
Few succeed
Prove to the mind that you will too.

Step three is to evaluate your
relationships.
Who do you influence and who influences
you?
Surround yourself with supporters.
A motley crew you inspire and who inspire
too.
Speak and have conversation.
Don't be afraid to challenge the narration.
It's ok to not agree.
This choice to deny only makes you more
free.

Step four is to repeat steps one through
three.
Because this way requires consistency.
A warrior that trains to the ultimate
degree,
in mind, body, spirit.
That's the way that I see.

Experiences

Life plays out as a series of plots.
Recycled characters, stages and story arcs.
Events that don't correlate in the end.
Yet they do.
Through you.
A mold for the universe we live in.
The start of the dreams we build
Manifested into living art.
Designed to make us feel.

Cycles

When one ends another begins
Infinitely rolling
It never ends
Natural patterns of the universe
Celestial works in motion
All circles
Perfect and round
The master of rings
Humanity
Love & trauma
Our spherical drama
A blueprint for everything.

Ego

You were the first to think something
grand.
Don't you know I thought that too?
Who do you think you are?

A fool who thinks themselves wise.
Me, a wise fool.

Maybe the same idea but not the same
manifestation.
Just because your idea isn't novel doesn't
mean it can't change the nation.

Ego works in two different ways.
But all in all the concepts the same.

Me, can't get past insecurities.
Myself, can only exist if its unique.
I, alone and weak.

Misconceptions of the inner we seek.

Moments

Glimpses of time.
We think them so ordinary but when we
really focus we observe that all are
extraordinary.

Missing the point.
Every-one is brand new.
From the morning silence to the afternoon
news.
To chatting old ladies drinking their blue
hued booze.

Chemical processes to interpret these
views.
The basis for moments, they get us to
move.
Living things we run on emotion, a fueled
feeling.
Bringing to motion.
Everything we know as true.

Frameworks

A universe so mysterious in design.
I swear all things must come from the
divine.
For aspects of Being creates the
foundation for everything.
These questions of how they come to be.

Does everything take shape through
efficiency?

Can we have a universe without a
principle of stability?

Why does the Earth have a molten core?

Is this something we know for sure?

How can it be that magma rises from the
sea to create these precious islands we
see?

Constant change yet the fabric remains
the same.

Is Change the mechanism for stability?
Counter-intuitive at first to me.

Is stability an aspect of maturation?

A goal of some sorts.
Harmony perhaps.
Maybe we all seek a particular frequency.
By tuning in we achieve consistency.
Self sufficiency
And stability
To get that much closer to Divinity.

Answers

What if I were to die?
What do I imagine an afterlife to be like?
Would it even exist?
Or do we become one with all?
Does our collective knowledge further
cement the physical law?

What if we are parasites to a living planet?
We suck life out of her, so she fights back.
Her immune system, designed to
eradicate on scales we cannot
comprehend.
Our destiny, to be wiped out in the end.
So she may begin again.

Who is God?
The condition of being needed.
They are the universe, the space between
every star.
The beginning and the end.
The answers and every question, lies
within them.

Divinity

Forever is my purpose.
Don't you realize how important it is to
transcend all that has ever been?

Beyond everything is nothing.
Something beckons above thee.
Never realize it is me.
For all things in between the fabrics of
reality.
Lies the threads of my living flesh
That God's greatest power is my own
death.

The Ego

An urge to be first and foremost.
To be excellent you must relinquish this
persona or be tormented by your need of
fulfillment.

Identity gets you to be great at higher
stakes.
High risk, insufficient reward.
Always chasing to get more.

Never being satisfied with the effort and
work that you provide, to thinking you're
the greatest alive.
Assuming things of other lives.
A mind trapped in the vortex of time.
Self-sustaining cycles of lies.

Refusing to understand who, what, when,
where, and why.
Because your pride is afraid to face your
mind.
And understand that all fears are just a
waste of time.

Reflections

The process of analyzing feelings.

Did we just do that?
Why?

I was caught up in the emotional high.
I didn't mean to say that did I?
Why did that happen to me?
Can't you see my suffering?
I need a reason to ease my mind.
So I look down into the pool.
See all the times I played the fool.
The waters can get deep.
It can seem like an eternity to get to where
the treasure sleeps.
The lessons to surface.
Only to provide further purpose.

Reflections Part I

Sometimes I can't tell if I'm projecting my insecurities on people or if they're doing it to me. Maybe we're doing it to each other. I don't know who I am half the time. One day I'm a thousand percent sure and other days I haven't a fucking clue. I smile all the time and I feel good, but sometimes I'm not sure if the smile is true. Like a true reflection of how I'm feeling that day. My thoughts sometimes exclaim that I'm the shit. Most of the time I feel like shit. Maybe not most of the time but you know what I mean. I be thinking the meanest things of the people I meet. I stress so hard because maybe that's just it. I'm a useless dirtbag who thinks nothing of the rest. Think the worst to make space for the best.

Connections

Our eyes meet
Yet I feel dismayed
Do I say "hey"
Or keep looking away?
I want to speak
Not sure if the words will reach
It might be too late but that's ok.
Another set looks my way.
I smile and wave
"How was your day?"
"Not bad, how about you?"
As if they care too.
Maybe they do.
Because secretly what we're after
are relationships that matter.

Who Am I?

Who are these strangers here beside me?
Like me they came to persevere through
their distractions.
Succeed?
If they have, I don't know
What I do know is that they're just like
you.
Someone I won't really know
So many things about you change
You are one thing today & another
tomorrow
I just want to know in this very moment
Just exactly who you are.

The identity ever changing.
Dynamic, as the rivers.
Never ending flow.
Never the same waters in the place you've
dipped your toes.

_Me?_

I used to dream of who I could be.
I used to play characters in each story.
Each scenario unraveling flawlessly.

My persona altered.
Constantly buffeted by insecurity and
desire.
Costumes would fail when the lines would
be altered.
From my mind to reality there was a
missing link.
The blame would always fall on me.
My insufficiency leaked.
You see I believed the deficiencies and
they became part of me.
Or at least who I thought I'd be.
A constructed identity.

Much more than it seems.
My being.
The true me.
Has always been there.
Wearing those silly costumes without
realizing the parts would be played
perfectly.
As the being that was always underneath.

Authenticity

Sometimes it's hard to feel good about
certain things.
Kind of scared to hurt some feelings.
You see I try to be the best I can be.
Whooped my own ass like a black belt of
the 2nd degree.
Being hard on yourself but not too hard is
that really trying at all?

What if I fall?

That's the reason you'll grow tall
Break down, stumble on the ground
Understand the depths of being.
It's easy to lose meaning
When you're constantly competing.
Have patience and listen to the beating.
So, you can understand the farther down
you go the more you can rest.
Assured that your soul will become its
best.

Reflections Part II

I can be insecure sometimes. I'm short, I don't know how to fight and all I know is how to wrestle rocks. For a time, I would get so jealous of other people. I would secretly hope people would fail and then pretend to feel bad in their face. So that I can be the one to succeed. As if their absence of success meant I couldn't be beat. I was constantly thinking other men were better than me. Taller, handsome, funnier, smarter, and harder working. Constant barrages to my psyche. It would all become jealousy, and my god it would blind me. Jealousy is one of the ugliest things. It doesn't discriminate between friend or foe. I didn't believe in myself so of course I would decide that anyone was better than me. If they were better than me how dare they not consider this injustice. It is not fair. They have all the advantages.

Confidence

Am I as good as I think?
These words bring me solace when I
speak.

Questioning my natural abilities will
strengthen my insecurities.

How do I really get better though?

Where do I want to go?

What do I have to show?

Be confident on the road you chose, and
the destination will be grandiose.

I know.

Insecurities

Easy to see the blemishes when you see
them so clearly.
Aiming for perfection.
A hard lesson.

These kinds of thoughts hold me like a
marionette.
A puppet of these perceptions.

I'm so ugly.
Weak.
Easy to beat.

My face burns with embarrassment.
How do I retreat?

These are the strings that bind me
and at the same time blind me.
To the reality that I'm preventing myself
from experiencing.

The presence of being.

Imposter Syndrome

There's a woman, whose beauty renders
knees to the ground.
I'm not speaking physically.
She's got a mind that is quite profound.
Her demeanor ordained by God itself.
She's brilliant, comedic, and masterful in
her expression.
Her heart is grand.
Tirelessly she works, honored and
revered.
Yet in her mind she fears.
She's not enough
For the standards imposed by us.
Even the best needs to step it up.
This is the culture where she was
cultivated.
One where she can't confide in herself
because she won't believe that she's
capable of all that she has done.

Jealousy

A beast whose visage even when masked
can't hide its repulsiveness.
It creeps into your thoughts.
Has the characteristics of bacteria.
Infects your mind until you can't decipher
reality from hysteria.

Jealousy pervades your heart.
It taints it with malice
Blinds your sight with anger and sadness.
What madness it produces.

This disease makes me very uneasy.
I can't believe how my heart deceives.
I need what I can't have.
Multifaceted conspiracy
He's so much better than me.
And you want him, clearly.

Probably don't even know who he is.
Probably don't even know who she is.
To jealousy they have shrouded intimacy.
Disseminated in my brain chemistry.

Approval

A degrading feeling.
The need to be fulfilled by attention.
It's called approval.
The only approval I need is mine.
When approval comes from other beings
who are fickle in their preference.
Then what value is that reference?
If it changes as the seasons through the
year.
Their values get cold through the winter.
Warm in the summer.
Therefore you will always suffer.
Straining yourself to find comfort.

This feeling that no one will like what I
have to say.
So be it.
The words will be free then.
No longer restricted by my inner
consciousness.
The self-conscious are restless.
Rest is the ultimate expression of
relaxation.
Relaxation harbors joy.

And my joy brings elation to the people I
love.
Be wary of the chains of approval.
They weigh heavy with your own heart's
disapproval.

Hope

Life's problems seem big, but they're as fragile as the twigs strewn across the forest floor.
What more can be said other than the mind is the wind that brings them down from the sky. Long for a time that we can see the clearing through the trees, feel the breeze, and live with ease.
Simplicity is privilege.
Being, clinging to a dream that is vivid.
Livid are those who can't see the flowers beneath their toes, too caught up admiring the flowers of their foes.
When their garden withers, so do their souls.
How can you grow when neglecting the seeds you sow?
Own yourself.
It's imperative for health.
Love is the only wealth that can be shared, with infinite to spare.

Reflections Part III

I act entitled sometimes. I know it.
Because when I want something bad it's
hard for me to take no for an answer. I'm
stubborn that way. But then I find myself
not acting that way all the time. It's only
when concerning other people. Like I
don't want them to have it if I can't have
it. Or I want something so bad I'll fight
hard for it but then change my mind once
I get it. Like what the fuck.... Why did I go
through all that effort to just sabotage or
take for granted what I wanted in the end?
Is that what Imposter syndrome is like or
is that just sociopathic tendencies? Nah
that's just being human, it's gotta be. We
are all animals and it's called competing.

Self-Served

Selfish in our pursuits no doubt
We truly wish to satisfy our own hearts.
Even those, who without a doubt.
Sacrifice themselves.
Separate themselves.
Share.
Ingraining themselves to others, their
pursuits, wishes, commands, and fears.

Selfish even in our selflessness
No such thing as selflessness
At least not in a world,
where one must breathe.

From Their Shoes

Their perspective
Almost adventurous in its essence
Only speculative in existence

I look determined
To ordain this leaf with some grace
Bestowed upon by my thoughts and
beliefs.
Or at least, that's my perspective.
Of their perception.

My ego exaggerates
Brings with it a delusion
That I am so entranced, even this
individual across from me cannot help but
gaze upon this illusion.

Conversation

Let's trade ideas since you see I know
nothing.
You know what you've seen.
I know nothing of those things.
You know the pain that you have felt.
I know nothing of the damage that was
dealt.
You know what is true for you.
I know nothing of the truth.
You know your hopes and dreams.
I know nothing of fate.
You know all your problems.
I know nothing of their answers.
You know your mistakes.
I know nothing of success.
You know your fears.
I know nothing of living.
You know what you believe about death.
I know nothing of what it's like to rest.

Mind Reader

A spirit siphoning my words.
I rack my mind to speak but the sounds
just won't come forth
An entity of fear to express the way that I
feel.
A dam of thoughts that will block my
promise
Of truth and sincerity, the foundation of
relationships.
The anxiety to speak my mind
How did it get this way?

The need to be a certain person.
Afraid to say something that can be
misinterpreted
But that comes from inside my brain
They don't know my lived experiences.
I don't know theirs.
So how is it fair to chastise words that
have no context.
The plight of reading minds.
Sometimes we think it's theirs but really
it's mine.

Expectations

Wouldn't it be easier to just wait patiently
for things to happen?
The nervousness and stress of what will
pass.
I don't know if I can last till it comes
around.
Because if it's not what I want then I'll
burn it all down.
How delusional was I to think that what I
envision is going to manifest?
Nothing is obligated to commitment.
In my mind some things are.
I can't help feeling disappointed.

Broad Aspects

Instead of neglecting the important
aspects of being human.
Play,
Compassion,
Love,
Humor,
Joy.
Place a broader focus on the real things
we enjoy.
For me it's been the pursuit of personal
growth.
From works to satisfaction.
Something to be learned.
The power to create has never left this
Earth.
While your mind trails off.
It waits for your return.
God creates life.
It's time to live yours.

Works

Everything I do is self-serving
I sat for hours learning nothing about you
and everything about me.
Not about who I can help or what I can do
to make things better.
Instead, I chose to sit down and write my
heart out.
All because I had nothing but time.
I'm better off scribbling letters for social
treasure than straining my wrist with
thoughts of who we are.

State of Confusion

Pride tied to lies or justified
The kind of mind
That can't decide
True or not
There's proof in thoughts.
Not to be cool or hot.
Claim to be wise or a fool.
Tool to be used.
By whom?
Self-serving is cruel.
The need is fueled by desires to please.
Please define what it means to rule over
yourself.
It's destroying my health.

People

When you read about the past,
The future is not all that bad.
We are creatures of habit.
After all, humanity is a species.
We make the same mistakes hoping for
different reasoning.
In a way it's hilarious to worry about
mistakes, people have already made them,
and we still refuse their takes.
On the exact situations we find ourselves
in today.
We have made progress though,
Slowly but surely, humanity is the
tortoise.
However, the hare is where we focus.
It's idolized.
Our culture has forgotten that evolution is
a process.
The human race.
The faster we go the longer it takes.

Candy Shop

There's a universe that exists that doesn't
have any defined limits.
It's special in the sense that it isn't.

A space like any other.
The inhabitants are qualities of a
magnitude we haven't uncovered.

These curiosities bring me great joy.
It wells up in the pit of my core.

Why that is?

I cannot comprehend.
Why the feeling of smallness makes me
feel so grand.

Part of me wishes to die.
So that I can finally understand the true
meaning of why.
In death it seems that all will be
presented.
There's just so many mysteries that
shroud existence.
For each question there are countless
answers and for each answer there are
countless questions.

There's no true path to life but if I had to
guess which to pick, I'm going on the one
that's yet to exist.
If I'm on it, who knows because if I'm
content with the road, the scenery will
grow.

The way to death is so intriguing to me.
It's like walking to the candy store.
Thinking I know what I want,
but when I get there, I find out there's
much more than I could've ever known.

All of them are distinct, variations of
delicacies.
Some bitter
Some sweet
Yet all of them are treats.
That must be what God sees,
The ruler of confectioneries.

Treeachers

I find the cold brings with it a serenity and
quiet beauty to behold.
A quilt of frost lays upon the wilting
branches of pines young and old.
Wearing proudly elegant coats of moss
Whose green hue glows with a purity that
God itself extolls.
Wondrous is the society of trees.
Whose community shows an abundance
of compassion and shared necessities.
Beings of incredible integrity.
Soothing is their presence.
When I'm lost it's their guidance I lean on.
Among their strong branches and earthly
scents.
I can make sense of the tangled strings of
existence.

Presence

Scrambled
Scattered
Tattered mind
Designed by internal infernal despise
A divine compromise

Teetering on the edge of sadness
Fall into the abyss
Darkness
Eroding the soul

Form takes place
Through the Universe's grace
Light & Space
Calm & Clarity
Despair & dread provided the charity

State of Being

Life in patterns
Internal matters
Slow and methodical
Fast and radical
To Summit all
Mathematical

Lost what's natural
Connection to the inner animal
Selection
Feelings are primal
Actualization
A deep sensation
Being is final.

Power of Communication

Words are magic
Sorcery that is phonetic

Elaborate
Thoughts and ideas can be prophetic.

Power so surreal
It's ability to make change is unreal

Influence
With your speech that's so fluent
Preach fire to it.
Spark and entire movement.

Guide

Will you please be the light of my dreams?
Because right now they're too dark to see
Each night before bed
I kneel and I pray
"Oh Universe,
Send me a magnificent array
Of the stories you display in our brains."
And each night they're too dim to relay
With you though
There's reliability that my mind will be
freed.
Through your lucid presence, dreams I
will see.

Writer

They say the pen is mightier than the
sword.
Mighty is a grand term.
Ruthless is more appropriate.
The pen has spilled much more.
Blood.
The sword doesn't produce ink, but the
pen does bleed.
Because of its inherent qualities.
It produces the laws of society.
Regimes rise and fall.
All this is the pen's fault.
Or is it the writers?
Who knew they could hold such power?

Kami

Master writer
Each line leaves wonder
The stroke of your pen
Is where reality begins
The story of creation gliding out as ink
Spills onto the sheet of infinity.

The plot for the wicked
Obsession with their image.

Freedom from possession of identity is
heaven.
With each atom to provide.
The lesson of the universe you designed.

Criticizing

Humans are truly creatures of infinite
potential.
The capacity to which we fear it, is quite
evidential.
We stifle each other.
Trample on mothers, sisters, fathers and
brothers.
Each one can change the course of
another.

My pessimism claims we'll tear each other
apart
Though potential has a funny way of being
art.
A piece of varying degrees
Optimism should be the lens through
which to see.
The masterpiece that is humanity.

Prayer

Let me begin by exclaiming that there are no words to truly describe the scope of your being lord universe.
As a mere creature of your living earth I can only exist in your image as a being of perfection contained in an imperfect suit of flesh.
The brain.
The mind.
The cerebral design.
Is the image you had this whole time.
Ape to human
The ability to think and create
It's incredible to cast our will into the world and watch it duplicate.
Our imagination is the universe you allowed us to rule.
The domain where all things are possible and plain as day.
The queue of dreams.
You designed it perfectly.
All within the skulls of our frames.
It took patience but you don't rush.
It's all in your timing.
Doesn't it make sense that humanity was created in their image.
The versatility, ingenuity, and creativity, it all derives from our cognitive ability.

We had to evolve from apes to be able to handle all the brain could take.
I am grateful for all the intricacies of reality.
Without you there would be nothing to exist.
Nothing to miss.

Words

Words are all that they'll ever be.
Thoughts, ideas, hopes, & dreams
Demons whose pursuits are fulfilled by
these vessels
Of characters & letters
Personalities & concepts
Tangible verses
Of promise and curses

Words are all that they'll ever be.
Packaged as a message
Through our inner divinity
Spirits manifested into physical forms of
art & beauty.
Eternal
Here we sit in a collection of journals
Written throughout the centuries.

I am, but one person
With ideas & a seeming sense of self
Who deems themselves righteous enough
to think that their words should be kept
through the years for all to read, analyze &
subject to their ears.

Or were these just ramblings
Of thoughts that plagued a mind
At that time, forever recorded.
Etched, ink & paper, for future
generations to find?

Words are all that they'll ever be.
Versatile is their pedigree.

Tools to purvey
Enthrall, enslave, seduce
Yet they can convey
Beauty, light, & radiant passion
That no other form can produce.

Words are all that they'll ever be.
Even in our loneliest days,
They keep us company.

Satisfaction

It's the underlying theme of all these
words
It's at the end, but not always.
Motivations exhausted with satisfaction
Fulfilled, no longer empty or longing
Today I feel complete
Today I feel established
With a relentless mind and
Ink in hand, we relished.

Tomorrow?
Who will I be?
Just like you?
In the moment we shall see.
What I do know
The greatest philosophy.
Is a belief in yourself with 100% certainty
and infinite possibilities are a fact of
reality.